FIFE EDUCATION
COMMITTEE
KING'S ROAD P. SCHOOL
ROSYTH

At School

Gill Tanner and Tim Wood

Photographs by Maggie Murray

Illustrations by Mark Peppé

A & C Black · London

Here are some of the people you will meet in this book.

The Miller Family in 1990

The Grant Family in 1960

Tony Miller is the same age as you.
His sister, Jane, is eight years old.
What is Tony's mum called?

This is Tony's mum, Helen,
when she was nine years old, in 1960.
She is with her mum and dad,
her brother and her baby sister.

The Brown Family in 1930

The Jennings Family in 1900

This is Tony's granny, Rose,
when she was just a baby, in 1930.
Her brother, John, is looking after her.

This is Tony's great grandma, Victoria,
when she was six years old, in 1900.
Can you see what her brothers and
her sister are called?

Can you spot the differences between these two classrooms?

One shows a classroom
in a modern school
and one shows a classroom
one hundred years ago.

This book is about school.

It will help you find out
how school has changed
in the last hundred years.

There are lots of mystery objects in this book
and you can find out what they are.
They will tell you a lot about people in the past.

One hundred years ago,
Victoria and Sam Jennings saw these objects every day at school.
Who do you think sat here?

Turn the page to find out.

This is Victoria and Sam's classroom one hundred years ago.
Can you find the mystery objects in this picture?
They are a **teacher's desk and chair**.
The teacher sat high up at the front of the class
so she could see that everyone was working hard.
In those days children had to work silently at their desks.
They only got up when the teacher called them.

Sam and Victoria used these things in their lessons.
The biggest mystery object
is about the same size as this book.

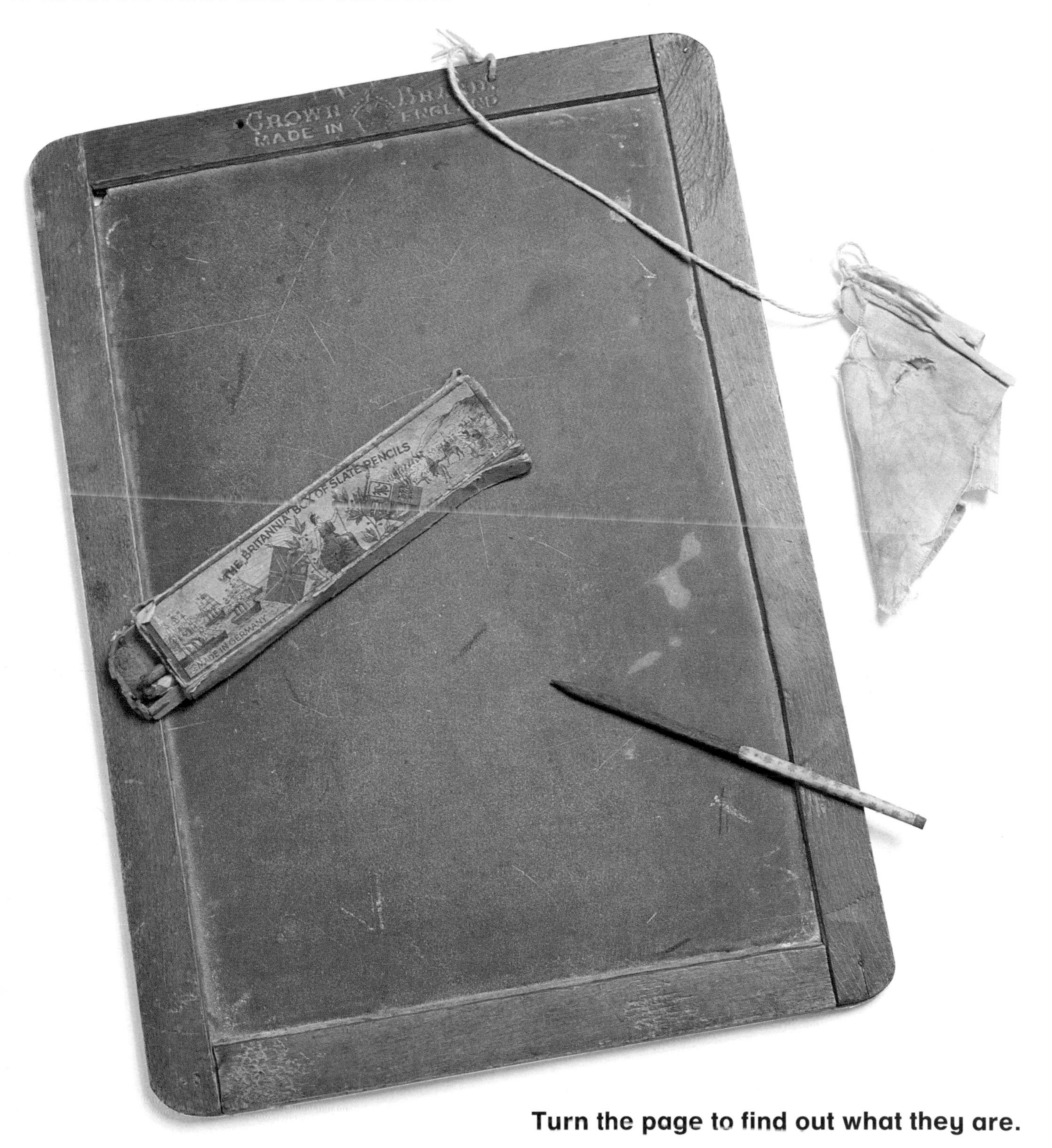

Turn the page to find out what they are.

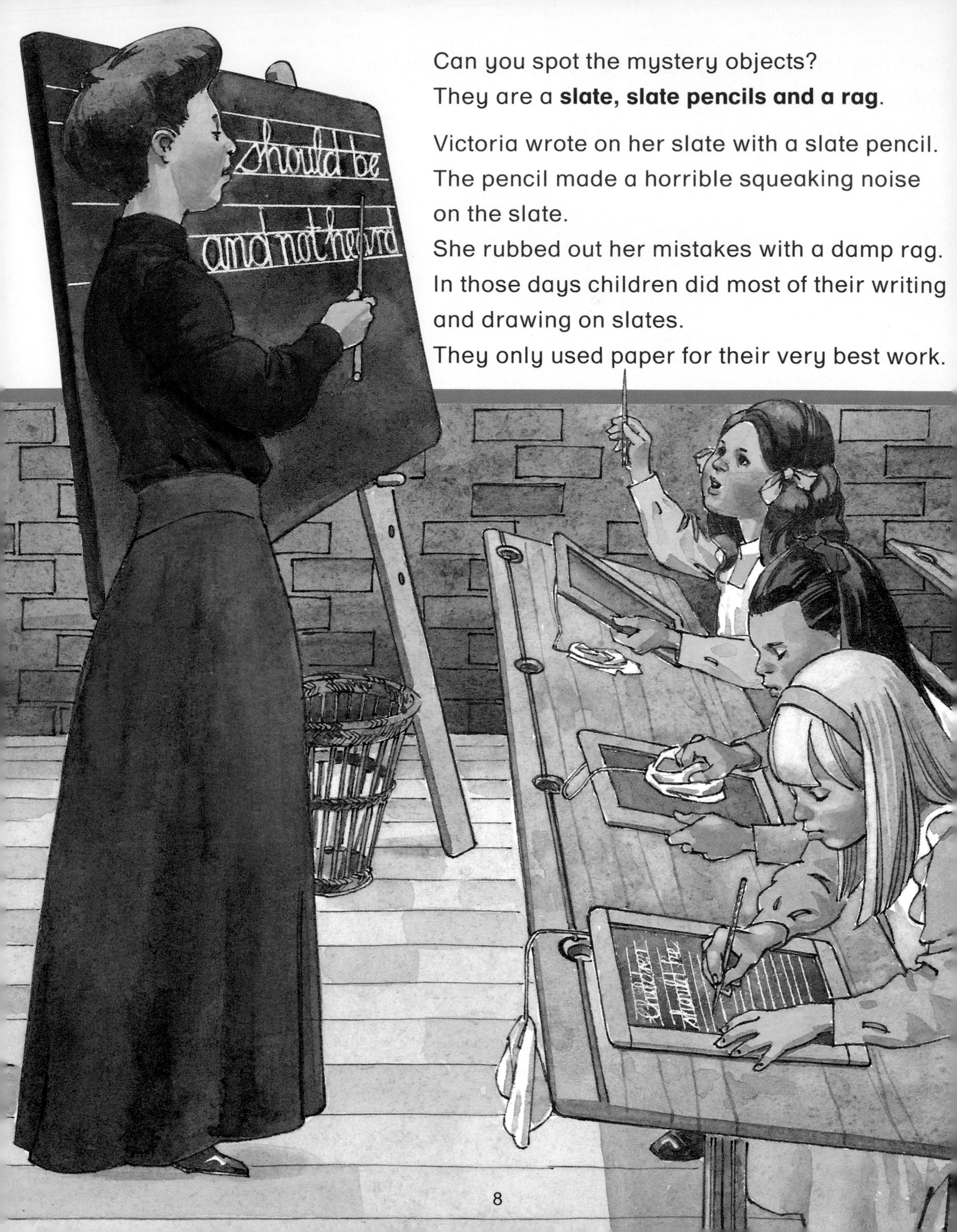

Can you spot the mystery objects?
They are a **slate, slate pencils and a rag**.

Victoria wrote on her slate with a slate pencil.
The pencil made a horrible squeaking noise on the slate.
She rubbed out her mistakes with a damp rag.
In those days children did most of their writing and drawing on slates.
They only used paper for their very best work.

The mystery object is a bit bigger than this book.
What do you think it is made of?
What do you think it was used for?

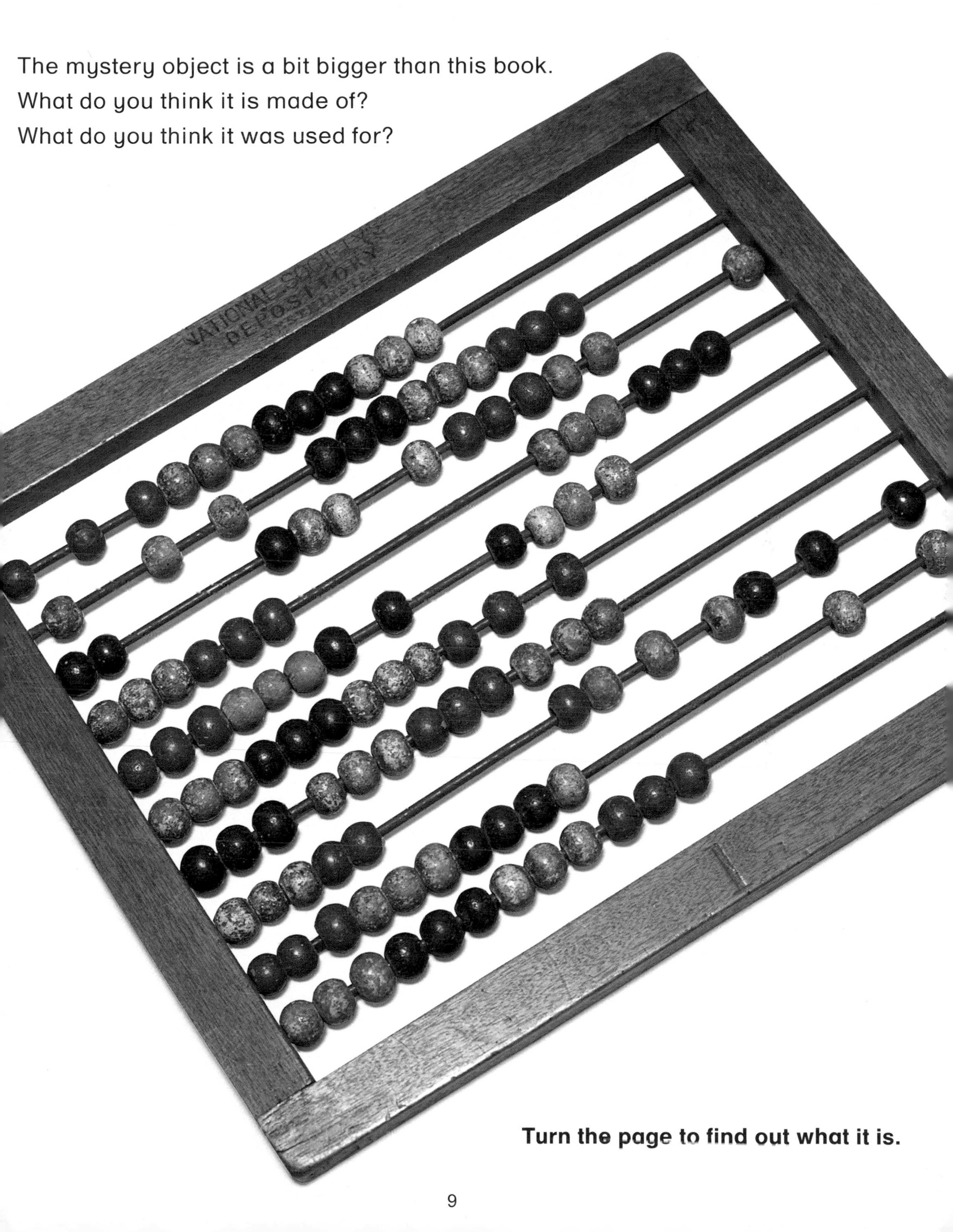

Turn the page to find out what it is.

The mystery object is called an **abacus**.
Children in Victoria's class learned to count with it.
The wooden beads stand for numbers.
Children did sums by sliding beads along the metal rods.

Some of the younger children did their sums in a sand tray.
They wrote in the sand with their fingers.
All the children learned to chant their tables out loud.

There are lots of mystery objects in this picture.
They were used in Emma Brown's classroom
in 1930.
Can you guess what they are?

The wooden tray is about the same size
as this book when it is open.

The object which looks a bit like a teapot was used
for pouring something into the little pots.

**Turn the page to find out
what these objects are.**

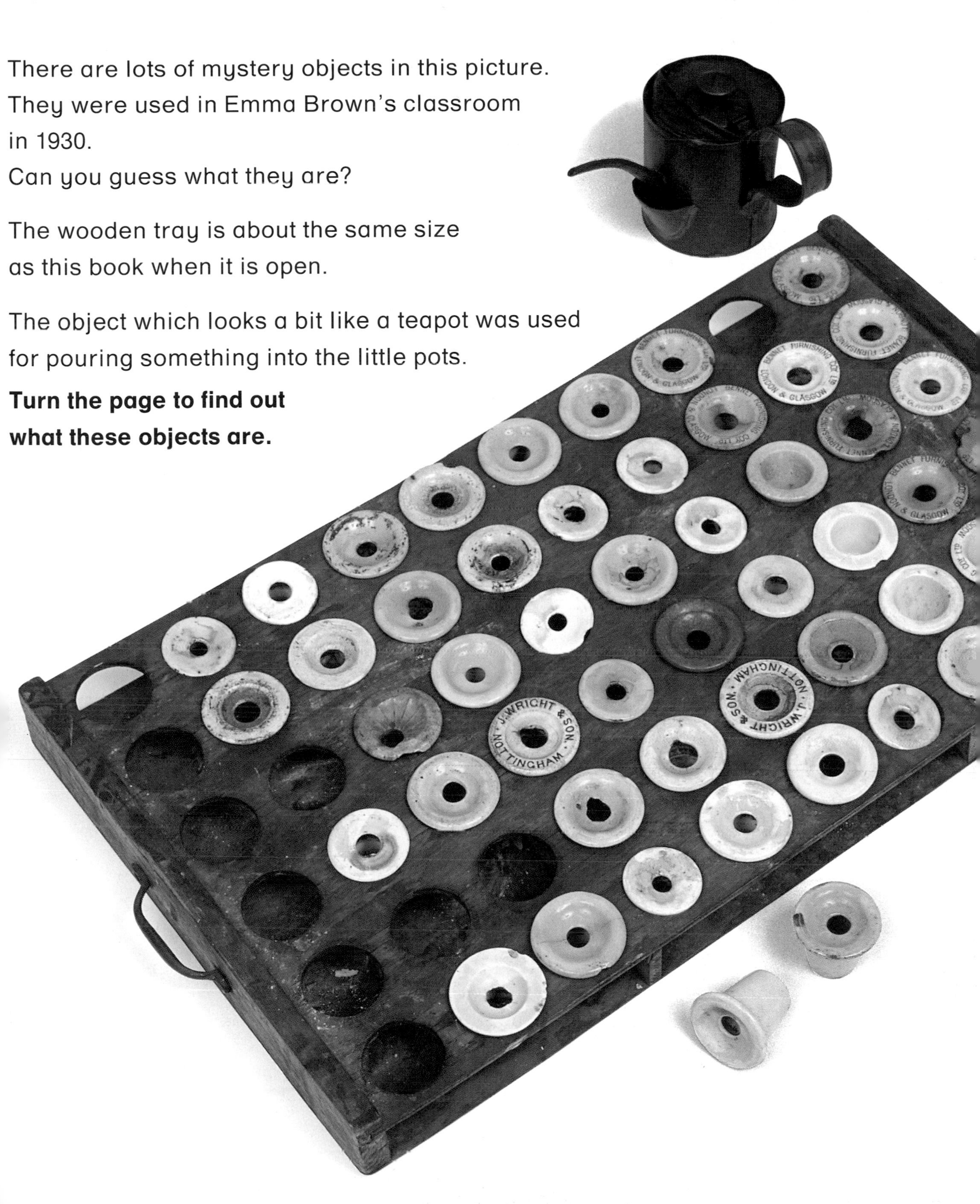

This is Emma Brown's classroom in 1930.
How is it different from your classroom?
Can you spot the mystery objects?
They are an **ink-can**, and **ink-wells**
in a **wooden tray**.

Emma Brown was ink monitor.
She came early to school every day to fill the ink-wells.
She put the ink-wells into the tray and carried them round the classroom.
She put one ink-well into a hole in each desk.
The children wrote with pens which they dipped into the ink.

John Brown used these mystery objects at his school.

Have you ever seen anything like them?
What do you think they are?
When do you think John used them?

Turn the page to find out.

The mystery objects are a **bottle of milk** and a **straw**.
Some children in John Brown's school
were given milk to drink at playtime.

The milk came in small bottles with cardboard tops.
The straws the children used were made of real straw

This mystery object is about the same size as this book.
It is a box with some cards and other things in it.
Can you work out what each thing is?
What do you think is written on the cards?
What do you think the mystery object
was used for?

Turn the page to find out.

Can you spot the mystery object?
It's a **word and sort box**.

John used it to help him learn to read.
He took the things out of the box
and then found the right card for each one.
The teacher checked his answers.
Did you learn to read like this?

The mystery object is about the same size
as this book when it is open.
Helen Grant used it at school in 1960.
Can you guess what it's made of?
What did she use it for?

Turn the page to find out.

This is Helen Grant's school in 1960.
How is it different from her mother's school?
Can you spot the mystery object?
It's a leather **satchel**.
Helen carried her books, pencils and lunch
to school in her satchel.
What do you carry your school things in?

This mystery object is about the same size as a small suitcase.
It works by electricity.
In your home you may have something like it, but smaller.
What do you think it was used for in school?

Turn the page to find out.

The mystery object is a **tape recorder**.
It was bigger than a modern cassette player.
The recording tape was not stored neatly in a cassette
but had to be wound round big plastic reels.

The teacher recorded programmes from the radio.
This was quite a new idea in those days.
The teacher used the programmes to teach
music and movement in the hall.

Now that you know a bit more about schools
and how they have changed over the last hundred years,
see if you can guess what these mystery objects are.
They are made of wood.
They were used by Victoria at school.
What do you think they were for?

You will find the answer on page 24.

Time-line

These pages show you the objects in this book and the objects which we use in school nowadays.

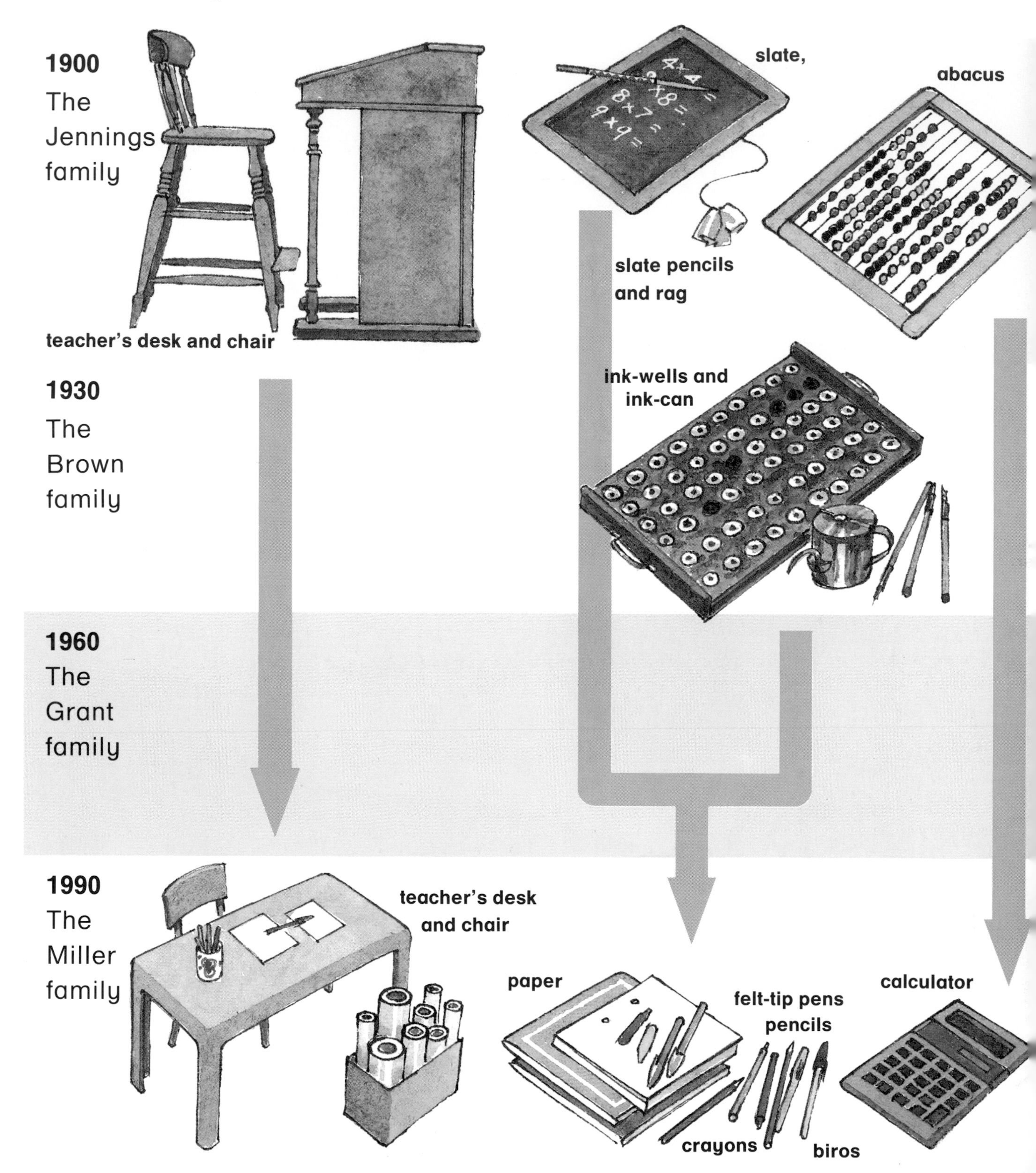

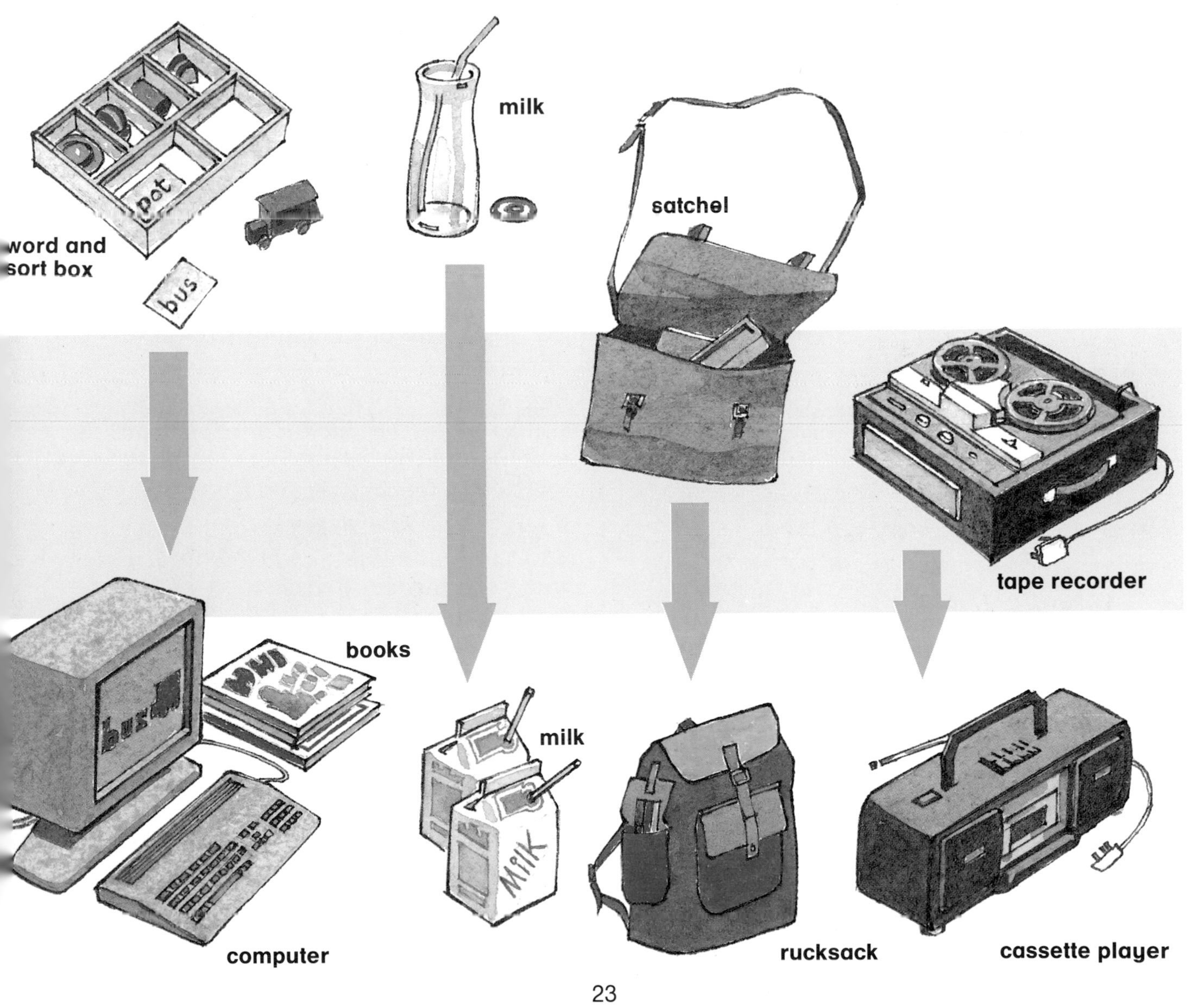
milk
satchel
word and
sort box
pot
bus
tape recorder
books
milk
Milk
computer
rucksack
cassette player

Index

The **mystery objects** on page 21 were **wooden dumb bells** used when Victoria Jennings was a child. Children held them while they did exercises in P.E. lessons, to strengthen their arms.

For parents and teachers

More about the objects and pictures in this book

Pages 5/6 In 1870, the government took over responsibility for education and soon made elementary education compulsory. By 1900, State elementary schools were free and the school leaving age was 12. Classes were often large, with girls and boys of different ages.

Pages 7/8 One hundred years ago, elementary education concentrated on the '3 Rs'. Teachers were paid by their pupils' results at the annual inspection, so discipline was fierce. Children were taught mainly what was to be examined and were drilled to answer parrot fashion.

Pages 9/10 More formal written maths schemes replaced the abacus after 1900.

Pages 11/12 The 1902 Education Act introduced secondary schools. By 1930, the school leaving age was 14. The fountain pen was invented in 1656 but cheap, mass-produced pens were not available until the 1950s. Dip pens and inkwells vanished with the appearance of cheap ballpoint pens in the 1960s.

Pages 13/14 By 1930, primary school children had free medical inspections at school, and those from poorer homes were entitled to free meals and free milk.

Pages 15/16 By 1930, lessons were more informal but subjects were differentiated with set times for arithmetic, reading, history, geography and nature study.

Pages 17/18 The 1944 Education Act made education compulsory and free up to 15. Many new 'open plan' schools were built during the '60s. In primary schools, desks were no longer arranged in rows and classrooms had more books and displays.

Pages 19/20 Recorders with plastic tape (invented in 1935) were not in general use until the '50s. Before this, programmes could only be used at the time they were broadcast.

Things to do

History Mysteries will provide an excellent starting point for all kinds of history work. There are a lot of general ideas which can be drawn out of the pictures, particularly in relation to the way schools, clothes, family size and lifestyles have changed in the last 100 years. Below are some starting points and ideas for follow up activities:

1 Work on families and family trees can be developed from the family on pages 2/3, bearing in mind that many children do not come from two-parent, nuclear families. Why do the families in the books have different surnames even though they are related? How have their clothes and hair styles changed over time?

2 Find out more about schools in the past from a variety of sources, including interviews with older people in the community, books, documents such as school log books and admissions registers from your local Records Office, and from local schools. School wasn't the same for everyone. Why not?

3 There is one object which is in one picture of the 1900s, one picture of the 1930s, and one picture of the 1960s. Can you find it?

4 Try teaching a Victorian lesson.

5 Look at the difference between the photographs and the illustrations in this book. What different kinds of things can they tell you?

6 Make your own collection of school objects or pictures. You can build up an archive or school museum over several years by encouraging children to bring in old objects, collecting unwanted items from parents, collecting from junk shops and jumble sales. You may also be able to borrow handling collections from your local museum or library service.

7 Encouraging the children to look at the objects is a useful start, but they will get more out of this if you organise some practical activities which help to develop their powers of observation. These might include drawing the objects, describing an object to another child who must then pick out the object from the collection, or writing descriptions of the objects for labels or for catalogue cards.

8 Encourage the children to answer questions. What do the objects look and feel like? What are they made of? What were they used for? Who made them? What makes them work? How old are they? How could you find out more about them? Do they do the job they are supposed to do?

9 What do the objects tell us about the people who used them? Children might do some writing, drawing or role play, imagining themselves as the owners of different objects.

10 Children might find a mystery object in their own house or school for the others to draw, write about and identify. Children can compare the objects in the book with objects in their own homes or school.

11 If you have an exhibition, try pairing old objects with their nearest modern counterparts. Talk about each pair. Some useful questions might be: How can you tell which is older? Which objects have changed most over time? Why? What do you think of the older objects? What would people have thought of them when they were new? Can you test how well the objects work? Is the modern version better than the older version?

12 Make a time-line using your objects. You might find the time-line at the back of this book useful. You could include pictures in your time-line and other markers to help the children gain a sense of chronology. Use your time-line to bring out the elements of *change* (eg. the gradual development of ballpoint pens and the use of computers) and *continuity* (eg. basic similarities in the processes of teaching and learning, and the need for schools, classrooms and teachers).

First published 1992
A & C Black (Publishers) Limited
35 Bedford Row, London WC1R 4JH

ISBN 0-7136-3490-1

© 1992 A & C Black (Publishers) Limited

Reprinted 1992, 1993, 1996

A CIP catalogue record of this book is available from
The British Library.

Acknowledgements
The authors and publishers would like to thank Suella Postles and staff
of Brewhouse Yard Museum (Nottingham),
Ruddington Local History Society Village Museum (Ruddington, Notts)
Mrs Tanner's Tangible History.

All rights reserved. No part of this publication may be
reproduced in any form or by any means - graphic, electronic
or mechanical, including photocopying, recording, taping or
information storage and retrieval systems - without the prior
permission in writing of the publishers.

Filmset by August Filmsetting, Haydock, St Helens
Printed and bound in Italy by L.E.G.O.